DIFFERENT PERSPECTIVES

SEHAR RASHID

Contents

Contents

Preface

Writing has been a part of my life since I was quite young. Being an introvert my lonliness made me a friend- paper. And even I didn't realise, when that friendship turned into passion. I can describe how happy I feel while writing, it,s my pen which makes me truly myself. Now talking about the book Different Perspectives, it is a poetry collection which includes the poems I simply wrote after watching something or feeling something.

HAPPY READING!

1. MY DREAM OF A DIFFERENT WORLD

I've seen a beautiful dream of a beautiful world,
Where everyone is free and no one is hurled
No child is seen doing labour,
And there's love among whole neighbour,
There's one thing between countries and that's peace,
The hearts of people are soft like cheese,
At the end of the day no table is left without meal,
People love each other and help others to heal,
There's harmony in people of every religion
Now people don't talk about their division
There's no difference between a boy and a girl
All are allowed to shine like pearl,
Rich or poor, everyone is equal before law
And no one can get away from its paw,
Oh! This dream is one of the best,
Everything in it feels like fest,
I hope this dream gets fulfilled soon,
And this'll be the biggest boon

2. SOCIETAL STANDARDS FOR MEN

I've seen men crying, yes they do,
But why society has made their crying a big issue
Men don't cry because they need to show strongness
who told you that crying is a sign of weakness?
resisting cry can make one's once mental health worsen
Crying just shows the emotions of a person
who says men don't feel the pain
not feeling it doesn't give any gain
Boys must be Harsh they need to be bossy
Who told you that this will look classy
I have seen men with soft behaviour
and their behaviour acts like a saviour
I have seen men who are happy in their lives
along with their families
I don't say that everyone is thinking like this
but a huge part of society is
time to change our thought
let's bring the change which needs to be brought

3. INCOMPARABLE LOVE

The first time I dreamed I was in my mother's lap
and it was my father who prepared my dreams map
they both taught me how to walk, talk and eat
their love for me is something which no one can beat
they told me the true meaning of education
and how it is one of the greatest creation
my mom always cooked my favourite food
and my father spoiled me with every little thing he could
my mom wanted me to be happy at any cost
my father hated my tears the most
they never stopped me from doing anything I want
"but I shouldn't do something wrong", they also warned
the amount of sacrifices they have made
no matter what I do they can never be paid
their love is something which no tool can measure
and being with them gives a great pleasure

4. FEMINISM:- A MYTH?

Are we making feminism a myth?
This is the topic I'm gonna start with,
At the time when we need equality,
We filled our minds with partiality,
Feminism started out as a help for women,
That was okay, but it's wrong to degrade men,
There were times when women weren't treated properly,
Then we spoiled the idea of feminism,
Wasn't it too early,
I know women suffers from a lot still,
But its wrong to make others pay the bill,
We made feminism a myth, were we so lost in pride,
Calm down, we need to think from every side
Fussing over a problem doesn't give a solution
to solve it we need to keep aside the commotion
first we should understand it all
and then make the actual call
All our acts should be with maturity,
what we should believe on is equality.

5. YOUTH RANGE FOR A CHANGE

Youth power can make a change ,
Today most of us think that everything's out range
Knowing we are the future of the country
We are afraid just to break that so called boundary
They can tie your body not your mind,
Don't forget you are a new hope for mankind
There are many values which we need to keep in ourselves
Keep those values with you otherwise you won't have
anything else,
Let your mind think what it wants,
And that will be the start of many new plants,
Don't think you are any less
Cause you can finish a lot of mess,
You have a power time to realize it,
Come on it's not just a little bit.

6. LAW VERSUS INFLUENTIAL PEOPLE

Since ages we've been reading "everybody's equal before law"
But time made realise that money and influence can get away from its paw,
Stop playing with law it's not a game,
People are suffering because of it, have some shame
A culprit gets saved because he is rich
so when are we going to fix this glitch
Because of this the victim suffers a lot,
People make him a laughing stock, even when he is not
Aarav a young boy
Lost his life due to an influential guy,
Not just Aarav we see many cases,
Of such people on a weekly basis,
And these problems are increasing with each passing day,
But we are just sitting and hoping for a ray,
now it's time to take a stand
And tie those people's hand

Time to make everyone equal before law
So that no one can get away from its paw.

7. OUR AIM IS EQUALITY

Let's tell young boys that crying is not a sign of their weakness,
Let's tell young girls that they will get nothing through their meekness,
Teach your girls to stand against the wrong,
Teach your boys to stand against the wrong,
Teach them that wrong doesn't have a gender,
Now we have to be the mender,
Cooking is not just a woman's job,
It's a profession in which both can hop,
Women aren't defined by weakness
And all men aren't the symbol of strongness
When a woman can get maternity leaves,
Then normalize men taking paternity leaves,
Teach men that raising a child isn't done only by fulfilling their economic needs,
Their emotional and mental needs are also necessary on which we should pay heed,
Stop setting standards of men with broad chests and women with slim bodies,

They both are human and they can have same hobbies,
Remember our aim is equality,
Neither matriarchy nor patriarchy.

• 9 •

8. RELIGIOUS DIFFERENCES

If your mind says that the person following other religion is
bad,
Then this is the thought about which you should be sad,
These diversions in religion can make our country suffer a lot,
If you trust much on media and think everything they show is
true, then time to realise that it's not,
And what are you doing shipping a specific religion with
terrorism,
Remember those who are terrorists don't have any religion,
So get out of this thought's prism
Eid is the festival of brotherhood, Diwali is the festival of
light,
But no religion teaches us to pick an unnecessary fight,
our religion teachers peace, compassion, kindness and
harmony,
When will we get bored of this Hindu Muslim monotony,
Did we forget that the British used the principle of divide and
rule,
If not then why we are forgetting our unity and being so
rude,

Are our bonds so weak that a little misunderstanding can
break us apart,
And hearing anything from anyone can make our emotions
depart,
Now be still for a minute and think a bit,
There still time to realise all of it.

9. THE WORLD OF MY IMAGINATION

The world of my imagination,
Which is a beautiful creation,
Where people support right rather than supporting men or
women,
And proper manners are taught to both of them,
Where a person sees another person as a human not a
person from another religion,
Where education is necessary and everyone is getting it,
And people don't think of it as a bit,
Where there are lesser differences in hearts,
And when called for help there aren't any ifs or buts,
Where anyone can live without any fear,
And people treat every person as their dear,
No wall of ego is stopping them,
They help each other as much as they can,
Where there are no wars and blood shed,
And white prevails not red,
They don't know the meaning of poverty,
Cause they know what's humanity,
Where parents and children share a lesser generation gap,

Children don't forget that they have played in their parents'
lap,
If actual word becomes like this,
Won't it be a huge bliss.

10. APPRECIATING LITTLE THINGS

Little troubles make us appreciate little things,
Cause we don't know what life brings,
Like a clear nose when you have a blocked one,
A little blow of wind when you are burning from the Sun,
A drop of water when you are tired,
That old job of yours when you are fired,
A Pinch of food when you are starving,
Those happy moments when you are crying,
The healthy times when you are unwell,
Your freedom when you are stuck in a cell,
The words of your parents when you are lost,
That's what you remember sometimes the most,
Tired eyes makes you remember sleep,
And when you get late you appreciate that morning beep,
Little troubles make us appreciate little things,
Cause we don't know what life brings.

11. WHERE IS YOUR HUMANITY?

Dear humans we didn't forget animality,
But being humans you forgot humanity,
You never get bored by killing dogs on the road,
You call us cute but snatched away our ice,
We request you to stop playing with nature's dice,
You kill Sharks in the ocean,
And you are talking about a better world's notion,
Why you snatch rhino's horn,
Understand that your selfishness is a thorn,
Killing deers just for the sake of their mist,
Stop! you need to control your fist,
Cutting our forests down,
Remember home is home and everyone loves their town,
Taking away elephant's teeth,
Which shakes him till last breath,
Humans, humans where is your humanity,
Why are you going towards insanity.

12. YOU'RE BEAUTIFUL

"I am so dark, I will try this fairness cream,
Looking fair has become my only dream"
Stop thinking like this,
Your skin is beautiful just the way it is,
Remember white rose is everywhere,
But only black rose is rare,
"Do something about your complexion its so dark"
Never let these talks take away your spark,
The actual beauty lies in our heart,
Let them be they won't understand this but,
Morning is beautiful so is night,
Never stop yourself from shining bright,
The colour of your skin doesn't define you,
And this is the fact which is actually true.

13. DARK AND LIGHT DIFFERENCES, STILL PREVAILING

Oh! She has such a dark skin,
She should know that only whites win,
You should try this fairness cream,
Otherwise living a good life will just be a dream".
"Is it true,
I started doubting myself because of you".
I feel it is astonishing ,
Dark and light difference still prevailing,
When we are living in a modern society,
And now we're attaining more and more modernity,
Every colour is beautiful,
Let's make a difference which is fruitful,
I'm dark or light skinned, I'm a person first,
Understand the fact, because now you must.

14. WANT TO BE A CHILD AGAIN

Can I be a child again,
Cause all things aren't the same,
And it seems a huge loss,
Even I am not the same person anymore,
And that hurts me to the core,
Can I go back to my childhood?
Where everything was so good,
Little things could make me happy,
But now everything feels so crappy,
It feels as I am stuck in a huge trap,
And I am also not able to find the map,
Can I turn the cycle of time once?
So that I can get another chance,
Just one to live those days,
Are there any ways,
Can I just be a child again,
Who can enjoy every game.

15. A LETTER TO 5 YEAR OLD ME

Dear little me,

Be what you want to be,

Enjoy your childhood,

It's the only thing which is good,

It's a precious time,

Don't waste it just on rhyme,

You are much more than being good or bad,

So there's no need to be sad,

Don't bound your mind with society,

It limits your prosperity,

Let your mind think freely,

Focus on what you want completely,

Don't trust on people on what they show,

Sometimes they can cheat you on the go,

Make a good relation with your parents,

They'll always be there for your reference,

Just do what your mind loves to do,

Be the true you.

16. LIFE

Why life is so strange,
That sometimes understanding it gets out of our range,
We usually ask others to live it,
But ourselves don't know a bit,
Sometimes it's full of sorrow and sometimes happiness,
Happiness is lovely but we can't get away from our sadness,
Childhood is the most beautiful part,
And as we enter adolescence it starts tearing us apart,
As we become a complete adult and get responsibilities on
our shoulder,
Our approach towards problems changes and we become
bolder,
Then comes the last phase,
Where we get wise enough to understand every case,
After sometime our breath stops and we depart,
And that tears our dear ones apart,
But once gone we can't be back again,
And here gets over the life's game.

17. CONFLICTING EMOTIONS

The sleepless nights,
And unnecessary fights,
I'm crazy everytime,
Whenever I try to rhyme,
I don't know how to get rid of it,
Can someone lessen this pain a bit,
I'm going on another shore,
Different from the things I adore,
The reason less crying,
And endless trying,
I want some rest,
To reach the best,
Oh! I'm so tired,
Feeling like I'm fired,
What to do,
Seek help, but from who,
I want to do this and that and all,
But I'm worried what if a fall,
My mind is full of commotions,
And I'm not able to understand my own emotions.

18.
RESPONSIBILITIES

Responsibilities are strange,
They make us do things even if they're out of our range,
It can make us do something we hate the most,
And sometimes while fulfilling them we find ourselves lost,
If we fail to achieve we are tagged as irresponsible,
People ask us to be more sensible,
They fail to realize that someone is Loosing himself in this
process,
While trying to complete every responsibility he posses,
The pressure one feels on his mind,
Is enough to make him bind.

19. FEELING LOST

Slowly, slowly I am losing interest in everything,
I don't know where am I going,
I am upset most of the times,
I don't even like the star that shines,
I'm feeling not to do anything,
Just sit there quietly and blink,
I want to sleep again and again,
Now I don't even enjoy the rain,
My head is filled with confusions,
And I am lost in my own illusions,
I feel like I am so alone,
And all my happiness is gone,
Like all my dreams are falling apart,
And I only wish this feeling to depart,
These thoughts are the worst,
"I am tired", I burst,
Like I am standing on a parted road,
And I don't know which way is good to go abroad,
And I am standing there all confused,
The decision making ability of my mind is diffused,
I don't know why I am lost,
And what it might cost.

20. LIKE DAWN

A new morning brings a new hope,
No matter how difficult it is to climb the rope,
Stand up and look carefully at the dawn,
Try to understand it and all your worries will be gone,
The sun which goes down in the evening,
Is the same sun which rises in the morning,
Only you know how difficult your life is,
And how deep are your bruises,
So you are the person who can make them heal,
Come on speak up what you feel,
Throw your fears away,
They are lying in your mind as hay,
It's time to glow like dawn as bright as that,
All your problems, now it's time to combat.

21. WILLINGNESS TO FLY

My dreams are like a shining sky,
I am a bird who want to fly,
I want to open up my Wings and fly,
As much as I could in the sky,
I'll break all the chains,
No they don't give me any gains,
I am a bird who is not meant to be in a cage,
Till now you haven't seen my rage,
You can't put off the fire inside me,
I will surely become what I want to be,
If you tie my hand I will break the rope,
Remember you can never kill my hope,
If you lock me up I'll break the door,
You can never shook me to the core,
I am like water you can't hold in hands,
I cannot be tied in your bands,
No matter how much you try you can't break water,
At the end you will have to hear my laughter,
One day I'll overcome my fear,
And it will be a victory which everyone has to hear.

22. NIGHTS

Nights are strange,
They trap us in our thought's cage,
Sometimes they become a cry time,
Sometimes a lovely rhyme,
All good ideas come at night,
And they make our eyes open up bright,
Sometimes they become so dark,
That kills our eye's spark,
When you are about to sleep,
A good idea comes in mind, beep,
And bam!
Half of your night becomes for slam,
You start making stories in your head,
Just by lying there in the bed,
Something that happened a long ago, oh I remember,
In that confrontation I should've given this answer,
I imagine the scene that never gonna happen,
And remember things that make me feels shaken,
All the motivation comes when I lie there,
Standing on stage, oh I'm successful so I'm here,
And the question comes what if I die,
How many people will cry,

A night becomes a wholesale stock of emotion,
And my mind gets filled with commotion,
Then I say shut up to my mind,
I've spoiled my night through thoughts of different kind.

23. SHE FEARS NO MORE

She was taught to be meek,
And they thought by doing so they can make her weak,
But they didn't knew,
That the storm inside her was enough to blew,
The fire inside her was burning,
And it kept on increasing,
With each and every wound,
They gave her by silencing her sound,
First she decided to overcome her fear,
Even when there was no one to hear,
Those who try to silence her gets shooked to the core,
Cause now she fears no more.

24. LACK OF UNDERSTANDING

I've a lot to say,
But the wall between us limits me every day
I can't say even if I want to,
I don't know what to do,
The wall of lack of understanding,
Which we keep on building,
Everytime we stand in front of each other,
And to me this difference does a lot of bother,
Maybe even you have something to say but can't,
A good bond between us even you want,
Ma, I'm your part,
And you're my heart,
But i don't know why I'm hesitated to share anything ,
Or am I scared what my talks might bring,
How to make things better I want to know,
The fear I have i want to let it go.

25. A MESSAGE FOR MY MOTHER

We might have differences in our thoughts,
But we don't have any in our hearts,
With you sometimes I fight,
But without you my life can't have any light,
Since childhood I have seen you caring for me,
I don't know if a good daughter I can be,
Even when I have to fight I don't lack,
Because I am lucky to have your back,
When I was ill you stayed awake the whole night,
The food was in front of you but you didn't take any bite,
I Know we don't share any ideal mother daughter bond,
But the love I have for you is so strong,
The generation gap between us can make us a little distant,
But you are the reason of my existence,
I've never seen a stronger woman than you,
I love you Maa, I really do.

26. HANDWRITING WOES

I was just seven,
When my teacher told me my handwriting wasn't even,
It was ignored that I was quite good at learning and
understanding,
When the fire that inside me was burning,
Was used to improved my handwriting,
And tragically , I failed even after fighting,
The notes with red pen kept on increasing,
And seeing that on my notebook my confidence kept on
decreasing,
I have tried many times,
Time passed I reached my nines,
I was always insulted for such bad works,
Why don't the understand it hurts,
I was in 9th class when a teacher came and called me dull in
front of mass,
That day I was shattered,
I felt it was just handwriting that mattered,
My self confident denied I started becoming an introvert,
They don't understand how badly it can hurt,

He didn't even know me how can he judge me just because
of my writing,
I passed my school along with lack of confidence,
And when I look back those days care me hence,
Handwriting is not a real judge,
Don't make it the way too much
Never kill the spirit of a child,
A student age is the most mild,
This shouldn't happen to any student
No one should feel what I felt.

27. FRIENDSHIP: A BEAUTIFUL RELATION [Dedicated to my best friend]

Friendship can be described in many ways,
It emits within us like sun's rays,
A friend is the one who stays with you in lows and highs,
He'll never tell you any lies,
The one who fights for you,
Is the one whom you can call true ,
He accepts you for who your are,
Who helps you overcome the bar,
With whom you can share your happiness and sadness,
You both are always together in every mess,
Doesn't matter how smart you are, he's never less,
Being with him life never seems complicated as chess,
The one who stand with you at your worst,
That's the person who deserves to be with you at your best,
Never loose that friend cause he's the real one,
Who'll always shine in your life as sun.

28. DRIVE AND DIVE

Drive and dive can be dangerous for you,

But I can't control your mind so what to do,

Diving into thoughts while I drive,

Even when I don't want I dive,

I get lost into my own world,

I don't need anyone to have a word,

All my loneliness is gone,

Even when I am thinking all alone,

The sea of thoughts is beautiful indeed,

After diving into it everything else I don't need,

I get out of my thoughts only to realize,

Too much thinking I should minimize,

Oh! My busy mind, I lost my way,

But paths seem familiar so there's a rat,

No, no, no I'm on the right road,

I needn't think too much instead I should get bored,

Otherwise one day I'll actually loose my way,

And then there might not be any ray.

29. PAPER: A GREAT FRIEND

The much I write,
The more my eyes get bright,
The happiness I feel,
Makes every pain heal,
The smile on my face,
Gives me a different grace,
I wrote when I felt alone,
And all my sadness is gone,
That's how paper became a great friend,
Now I don't have to bother about any trend,
My closeness to paper is as such,
That I share everything but it never judge,
No matter how heavy my heart got,
It's lightness which it always brought,
When I have no one who'll hear,
My great friend paper was always there.

30. MY FIRST STAGE PERFORMANCE

It's always clear that I love to write,
I cannot even tell how it makes me feel bright,
After years of writing I decided to show my talent on the
stage,
But the stage fear I face has my rage,
Still I gathered some courage and went to an open mic event,
I prepared my few works for it as it really meant,
As soon as they called my name,
I felt like I was loosing the game,
I was trying to control but felt continuous shivering,
"Control yourself, it's easy", I was murmering,
Somehow I stood up and went to speak,
At that time my fears were at the peak,
I looked at the people who were looking back,
It was a feeling that my mind got some kind of hack,
Then I started reciting by looking at the poem in my hand,
And my confidence was slipping like sand,
After looking back at the audience I forgot everything,
I stopped in between and gave it a blink,
I was trying but couldn't complete my poem,

Somewhere my mind was saying come on show'em,
But I left it in between "thankyou" I said,
I came without completing that was my bad,
When I sat on my seat my body temperature got high,
They can do it so why can't I,
I don't know why I got so hopeless,
So much that I myself made it a huge mess,
I pronounced some word worst,
But no matter what first always remains first.

About The Author

Hi, I am Sehar Rashid.I'm a teenager [born 8-jul-2004]. I wrote two books earlier than this one titled 'The world of words' and 'Aarushi's teenage journey'. All my books mainly focuses on social issues. You can find me on instagram as Author Sehar Rashid @sehar_rashid_. I'll be pleased to talk to you guys and ofcourse I'll love to know your reviews.

Thankyou.